STRONGER CONNECTIONS
A Happier Life

Nurturing and Maintaining
Meaningful Relationships

ROSIE KENDALL

ISBN: 978-1-7397525-0-7 (paperback)
ISBN: 978-1-7397525-2-1 (eBook)

Credits
Book cover and layout design– Innovation Print

Printed in the United Kingdom

For enquiries, contact the author
Email: coachingwithrosie@gmail.com

To The Reader

Please note that the purpose for which this book is written, and its contents are solely based on the author's personal knowledge, experiences and conclusions, and interviewees involved, and it is only meant to act as an inspirational and motivational guide. The information and advice in this book whether provided in hardcopy or digitally are not intended as a substitute for any professional medical advice. Therefore, should readers wish to make any changes to their lives, they should seek the assistance of a qualified medical professional. The author has made all efforts to ensure that the information is precise; therefore, any errors that may exist will not be a liability to the author or publisher.

DEDICATION

———————

I would like to dedicate this book to Auntie Florence, who has been a great support since childhood to this day, and to all the readers of my books.

ACKNOWLEDGMENT

Sincere thanks to everyone who has allowed me to be part of their lives and maintained a strong connection.

I want to extend my gratitude to Vladimir K for their support during the time I was writing this book. I appreciate every second and minute of your time dedicated to me.

To Brigitte, for the time during the writing of this book, thanks for the inspiration and talks. To all the lovely people in the UK and USA who dedicated their time to me during the writing of this book.

I would like to thank the book cover artist and the editing team for putting this book together. I would like to thank all the interviewees; I appreciate you for allowing me to share your experience and story with others. Finally, I say a big thank you to all my readers. Your feedback has encouraged me to write more and share with you.

CONTENTS

"The quality of your life is the quality of your relationships"

— *Tony Robbins*

INTRODUCTION

The passion I have for life skills and coaching has inspired me to write this book. I hope to inspire and empower others by sharing my knowledge of life skills. Life skills are the essential skills we acquire to manage our day-to-day lives, and many areas fall under them. However, I have taken great interest in *'interacting with people'*.

My extensive travels have allowed me the opportunity to interact with people from many backgrounds in different countries. That's why I took great interest in how to interact with people so that I can build stronger connections.

What made interacting with people special for me was the fact that I had to apply understanding effectively to understand each individual in my interactions with them, and to better relate to them and enjoy my experiences with them.

Whether or not you enjoy travelling, understanding and being understood can allow you to interact with others more effectively no matter where you are. Interacting with others using life skills might mean nothing to someone who prefers to live in isolation and is comfortable just being by themselves. Interacting with the right people can take you further. With the right people, I mean people with good connections and good intentions to help you progress in life.

The social nature of humans requires interaction with other individuals. You may have one or more relationships you value, and relationships can't survive on their own. For these valued relationships to thrive, they need to be nurtured. We commonly focus most of our attention on our love relationships, but we have to also try to maintain other relationships we are a part of. By 'other relationships', I refer to relationships with friends, family, co-workers, etc. The complexity of the situations we may encounter in our lives can also affect our relationships in most cases. Therefore, in order to maintain its strength, it is necessary to continuously develop relationships.

Researchers have found that better health, greater happiness, and long life are associated with satisfying relationships (not just love relationships but also friendships, family, and our community.[1] This tells you that, the relationships we form have an impact on our lives, and being able to understand each other and nurturing healthy and meaningful relationships can impact us positively.

From my personal experience, and through the coaching of others, I have noticed that interacting well with others can contribute to our success. Applying life skills and interacting with others is vital because it impacts a very crucial part of our lives as it influences our decision-making, which also contributes to us making good or bad choices in life. Therefore, I believe that maintaining these relationships that we value can improve our quality of life.

The 2020 pandemic has not only brought a lot of distress but has also made us realise how important our relationships are. During the pandemic, people have approached me with broken relationships and the need for someone to talk to. Relationships may end for many reasons regardless of their form; however, this book focuses on those ends which could have been avoided. That is why I wrote this book, so you can see how vital life skills are, particularly in the area of understanding yourself and in interactions with others.

Throughout the book, the chapters serve as a guide to help you create and maintain stronger connections to impact your life positively.

I hope that this book will act as a guide for managing and strengthening your various relationships through the act of understanding. As part of this book, I have also included the experiences of other people I know in order to gain insight from other perspectives.

Who will this book benefit?

This book is for you if:

- You want to work on your authentic self

- You want to strengthen the relationship with yourself and others

- You want to discover strategies to form a meaningful relationship with yourself and others

- You want to work on effective communication with others

- You want to interact better with others

- You struggle to implement understanding in your life

- You feel disconnected from yourself or with others

- You are committed to personal growth

- You are looking to dig deeper into the power of understanding

How important is it for you to improve your relationships? Let us explore more on '*Understanding*' for building stronger connections!

CHAPTER 1

UNDERSTANDING YOURSELF

"Your relationship with yourself sets the tone for every other relationship you have"

— *Robert Holden*

*D*o you sometimes question why you are being misunderstood, whether you are at work, with family, friends, or even with a partner? It can be frustrating at times and quite difficult to deal with. This can also make you question yourself. Or have you thought about your process for selecting who to get close to within relationships? But have you wondered how well you are connected to yourself?

These are questions I had to answer once upon a time to make sure I was nurturing the right relationships for myself. To connect with others, it is first important to connect with yourself. So, understanding and accepting others depends on understanding ourselves first. It would be beneficial to you to discover and accept yourself as an individual. Here are some reasons why.

- It builds your confidence
- The love you have for yourself will reflect in your relationships
- It assists you in forming positive and meaningful relationships
- When you are an original version of yourself, you can interact with people more effectively

When it comes to getting the most out of anything, understanding is essential, and that goes for understanding yourself, too.

Let us start by looking into *'Self-Acceptance'* and how you can nurture your relationships by accepting your uniqueness.

What is Self-Acceptance?

Let me share with you how I define *self-acceptance*. Self-acceptance is the act of accepting yourself for who you are as an individual and this involves accepting both your strengths and weaknesses. When a person is able to recognize and accept themselves for who they are, they feel unique in their own way. Once we develop self-understanding, we begin to accept ourselves for who we are.

Accepting '*who we are*' does not have to only mean accepting our strengths. We also need to accept our weaknesses. It is a collection of attributes that make us who we are. All these give us something to work on so we can improve on our weaknesses and embrace our strengths. Self-acceptance is also about our general satisfaction with ourselves, which includes our lifestyle. By self-acceptance, I mean discovering, appreciating, and knowing the value of your unique qualities and worth, without the need to seek external validation.

One of the best gifts you can give yourself is the gift of embracing your uniqueness and one of the priorities and best forms for improving yourself is to start with accepting who you are.

What does this mean? We must accept who we are and embrace all that we stand for.

It is also important that we always show up as ourselves each day because no one understands us better than us. Even if some people aren't accepting of who you are, you should strive to focus on those who do. You stand a better chance of building relationships with people who can accept you as you are.

When you have a better understanding and acceptance of yourself, it can help you to interact with others and build stronger relationships. For instance, if you are aware and have accepted certain personality traits, you will know what you can tolerate from others. You can effectively manage your relationships with others by knowing who you are and managing them according to knowledge of yourself. As a result, whatever you accept will reflect your individuality.

Having said all this, have you accepted yourself entirely? Do you find that you are trying to convince yourself of who you are instead of working on improvements? Try to find out who you are and make a decision to accept it. Remember, everyone is unique. Let us delve deeper into the importance of self-acceptance and the differences it can make in our lives.

Importance of Self-Acceptance

Let's be honest, we live in a society where perfection is expected of us. Sometimes it makes it quite difficult to accept ourselves or our mistakes. We seem to be surrounded by standards of perfection. Psychologists Dr. Paul Hewitt and Dr. Gordon Flett identified three dimensions of perfectionism (1. Self-oriented perfectionism, 2. Other-oriented perfectionism, and 3. Socially prescribed perfectionism).[2] In the US and UK for instance, research shows that the perfectionism culture of the number of people experiencing three dimensions of perfectionism has been increasing since the mid-1990s.[3] This informs you about the rise in personal and social perfectionism. Perfectionism can impact your well-being and relationships; therefore, it would be helpful that we are realistic about our individuality.

It is common to have people around us who have high expectations of us and who they want us to be, even when it does not match our abilities, and this can be pressuring. Not having all great qualities is okay. What matters is that we accept ourselves for who we are. Self-acceptance is essential for our daily lives.

To identify parts of you, it's important to listen to yourself, and that will lead you to accept areas of your traits.[4] If you accept yourself for who you are, regardless of what you know about yourself, it will show in your personality and influence how other people perccive and treat you.

There's a lot that self-acceptance can do for you, like building your self-confidence and self-esteem. It would also aid in the development of identity because what we know about ourselves and what we accept about our identity is what binds us to our identity. That will make us believe in ourselves and not live according to how others want us to. We will most likely lose our identity the moment we live to please others. More so, it will be like having to get a new name, date of birth, etc., because a different person has been created. Our relationships require us to be true to ourselves.

Sometimes, if we do not improve certain aspects of ourselves, these traits will negatively impact our relationships with others. If we don't accept them, we can't work on them. Are there any characteristics that you can think of that can influence your relationships or interactions with others? Depending on what each individual may choose to improve on themselves in terms of personal development and growth or what they feel can make their lives better will ultimately impact them positively. However, this is all an individual preference. I say individual preference because the desire to make changes is all up to you. But the most important thing is that we understand the qualities we have; we know what effect these qualities have on our lives and how they impact our relationships with others.

Because no one is flawless, there's a significant chance that as time passes, you'll learn something new about yourself that has to be improved.

The important thing is to discover and accept them. If not, they do not feel real and every effort to make changes will be stifled.

In a non-acceptance situation, our self-esteem may be impacted, and we might seek validation from others because we may depend on what others might say and think about us and end up paying attention to what they say or believe about us. Because as mentioned earlier, trying to make an impact on something you have not accepted could mean you do not believe it to be true and will most likely be challenging. So, accepting traits about ourselves will be beneficial to our development as a person as well as to our relationships because as humans, we will need to constantly improve.

We are all a work in progress and therefore, will continually work on something to improve ourselves. Let me show you what it's like to achieve self-understanding and acceptance.

Achieving Self-Acceptance (i)

I have had the opportunity to speak with a few people who have shared their experiences on achieving self-acceptance. I spoke with two people to provide specific situations, which led them to take charge of their lives and improve their relationships with the help of self-acceptance.

>>>> *Please note that I specifically chose these two examples to show how self-acceptance can be achieved. Many examples can be connected to self-acceptance.* <<<

James's Experience

James has always been identified as the least smart one amongst his siblings. All his siblings have attained a bachelor's degree except him; however, he felt higher education was not his strength. Growing up, he had always been critical of himself and his achievements because his siblings were able to achieve certain things in life. Therefore, he felt that he should be able to achieve them also. James had spent many years feeling sorry for himself and became stressed about his future as he is unable to get an academic degree and live up to the expectations of his family. Self-pity has been a huge part of his life. James didn't have a good relationship with his family because he felt intimidated and worthless around them. To gain a better understanding of himself, James took an interest in self-understanding to discover who he was. It took him a while, but James has now accepted that furthering his education may not work for him as it did for his siblings. He has acknowledged that he has a unique passion and interests that he can explore. James has always had an interest in fixing things, and although he did not have a university degree like his siblings, he took a short certificate course and acquired the skills to become an electrician.

He is now happy, knowing that he was able to accept who he could become without accepting who others wanted him to be. He has learnt to build on his skills and focus on his talent, which is unique to him. He has learnt to be aware of who he was and what he could become and put that into practice to achieve his dreams. James is now living in alignment with his true self rather than trying to fit in. He has also improved on his relationship with himself and others as he is more content with his life, which in turn has positively impacted his relationships.

It could happen that there would be times in our lives when we see ourselves living according to the expectations of others. Most times, this happens when we are less confident. It's far from our reality and could make life difficult for us. How are you living now? Whatever you are doing now, is it something that you really want to do? Or is it something others want you to do? It's very important that whatever we are doing is what we want to do, and not to fulfil the expectations of others. We have to live out the consequences of the choices and decisions we make. This is why we need to be in charge of what we want to do and not do.

You are likely to come across people who are very interested in telling you what to do with your life, but it is up to you to make the choices that are right for you. There's nothing wrong with listening to advice if you wish to, but in the end, you get to decide what works best for you. Remember, you are in charge of your life unless you need assistance due to health or other reasons that are crucial to decision-making for special circumstances.

Vanessa's Experience

Vanessa expressed how she struggled with a relationship breakup. The healing process was long and very painful for her. According to Vanessa, although the breakup was a mutual decision, she never accepted their situation. She lived in denial by not accepting the situation as it was. This impacted her negatively as the way she felt led to other things, including low self-esteem, stress, anxiety, and loneliness as she could not cope with being around others. During that time, Vanessa avoided a lot of meaningful relationships. This went on for over a year, as stated by Vanessa until she realised, the only way to repair her self-worth is to accept the situation as it is. By accepting it, she was able to work on her recovery to achieve happiness again.

The very first step was to identify the situation and accept everything because non-acceptance could cause blockages or struggles to heal. For example, looking at Vanessa's experience, although most people will enter a relationship with the aim for something long-lasting, unfortunately in life, things happen that can change our lives and situations in ways we cannot imagine. There's nothing wrong with grieving a relationship that has ended as it's part of events that could happen in life, and I understand that everyone has their way of grieving. However, if grieving is consuming your life, then possibly it could be helpful to consider self-improvement. Is there anything that is preventing you from accepting the truth about yourself? If so, then how are you dealing with it to prevent you from negatively impacting the relationship with yourself or others? As stated earlier, if you are not your authentic self, it will surely show in the way you interact with others and you could end up missing out on a lot of meaningful relationships. Time can't change an event but can make a difference. Hold on tight and you will surely get there. Remember, healing is a process and one of the ways to get through it is with acceptance.

Another way to tell if you've achieved self-acceptance is to look in the mirror and accept all that makes you who you are. It can also show when you no longer try to mitigate others, ignore, or explain away any perceived faults or flaws, physical or otherwise.[5] By all means necessary, it is possible to achieve self-acceptance. It is necessary to identify what must be accepted and to commit to the process of attaining self-acceptance.

Action Tips

Achieving Self-Acceptance (ii)

Do you ever see yourself in a situation where you feel you are unable to move forward? While working towards self-acceptance, acknowledge that it is a process, and it may take time depending on each individual. However, I hope you can be prepared to go through the process organically.

Here are some scenarios linked to self-acceptance that we may find ourselves struggling with. Remember, how we feel about ourselves has an impact on our relationships; hence, we can improve our relationships by accepting ourselves.

• *Accepting your weight* – Most people have a preference for their ideal weight goal. It is just an individual preference, and every individual should be comfortable with a preference as to how they feel about themselves. Also, if you find yourself in a situation where losing weight could improve your health, I hope you can find the courage and motivation to accomplish your goals. If you are not comfortable with your weight for whatever reasons, it will help to first accept it and work on your ideal weight. You may discover that the starting process to achieving your goal weight will feel different in a good way, only because you have accepted it. It could also help battle procrastination and motivate you. Feel comfortable with yourself and work towards your goal.

● *Accepting your achievements* – Each person has probably accomplished something in life or is, at least, working towards something. Accept what you have now; you have come this far and worked hard for it. If you wish to work for more, go for it, but it is important to accept your current situation for what it is. This will be a good form of motivation. Be proud of yourself for every achievement and every goal you have accomplished.

● *Accepting your relationship status* – It is not a shame if you are single, and if you are divorced or separated. If your marriage is struggling, it's also not a shame. If you are experiencing difficulties in your relationship with friends, family, or co-workers, it's not a shame. No matter what your relationship status may be, the most important thing is to *accept* what it is and work towards your goal. Resisting acceptance will not help make any positive progress. It will be beneficial for us to accept that we will work towards change. Remember, no one's relationship is perfect, regardless of the form. Accept where you are and focus on where you wish to go with your relationship.

• *Accepting your uniqueness* – Accept everything about yourself; you are unique, and everything about you is special. Work on your talent and skills and whatever you want to improve. Your journey in life is unique, so there is no comparison to another person. Hence, no need to compete with others. It is also not necessary to feel you are above or below others. What might work for one person may not necessarily work for another. Everyone can't be in the same phase of their lives. We all have to take turns and wait for our time. Embrace yourself for who you are and stay focused.

• *Accepting your mistakes* – How we see mistakes can either negatively or positively impact us. Use your mistake as a lesson to better yourself and try not to become overwhelmed with self-criticism and self-judgment. Life doesn't come with instructions on what works and what doesn't, so our experiences with mistakes are part of the learning and growth process.

Ask yourself, what did I learn from this mistake? How can I use it to improve myself? That mistake will effectively teach you how to make improvements in your life. You will know what works and what doesn't work and gain the opportunity to explore better ways either for yourself or for your relationships. If the mistake is seen as a weakness, once you have decided to improve on it, it becomes 'a strength' and adds to your collection of strengths. Unfortunately, there are going to be people out there who will feel it's necessary to remind you of your mistakes, but that shouldn't affect you if you have already accepted them. Rather, it should give you control over how you feel when you encounter such situations. This is one way where self-acceptance builds your confidence.

Key Reminders

- The overall conclusion highlights that self-acceptance could have a positive impact on our lives.

- Self-understanding is one step, which can be followed by self-acceptance. One can explore various ways that would help overcome self-acceptance as part of the process to boost their quality of life.

- Accepting your weaknesses is just as important as accepting your strengths, as that gives you something to work on and allows self-improvement.

- Applying self-acceptance to your life will free you from being obstructed by unpleasant comments made by others about you, especially when you are aware of what needs to be worked on to improve yourself, which you have already identified. We can surely love ourselves better with minimal self-criticism.

- Self-acceptance can also make our relationships better with others because it allows us to be our true selves around others.

- Understanding ourselves and others is greatly enhanced by self-acceptance.

- Whatever you choose to accept about yourself is who you will become and what you accept to transform your lives into.

- If you don't feel good about who you are as a person, not accepting who you are or your situation, will impact how you behave around others and how others behave around you.

CHAPTER 2

UNDERSTANDING OTHERS

"When you get a better understanding of others, you become more open to developing better relationships"

Understanding others can be challenging sometimes. Do you ever find yourself in situations where you have difficulty understanding others? Have you ever wondered why people act or behave the way they do? This chapter will give you a good grasp of it and explores ways to be more understanding of others to nurture your relationships. In no part of this chapter or book does understanding others mean accepting or tolerating wrongful or harmful situations or behaviours that could pose a risk to a person, but rather just understanding their general ethos.

In what ways do you maintain the strength of your interactions with others? Most people will find that they live their day-to-day lives based on how they handle themselves and interact with others. It makes sense, therefore, for you to create a system that enables you to do this. We can increase our understanding of others to enhance our relationships with them and make them more meaningful.

When you get a better understanding of others, you become more open to developing better relationships.

Here are *seven ways* we can cultivate our understanding of others to strengthen our relationships, keeping in mind that just as understanding yourself is a journey, understanding others will be a journey as well.

1. Understand that People Change and Situations Change

Over time, certain things change for different people, and what we once knew about them might change. Just as you would undergo life changes, so do others. People change their minds, lives, situations, and even ways of doing things. Therefore, being open-minded and communicating regularly would benefit our relationships. Thus, we need to update ourselves with each other frequently to know where people are in their lives. It would be beneficial for you to pay careful attention to others when interacting with them. Giving your full attention to others during interactions can help you understand them better and help you be present.

2. Applying Approaches to Understanding

(Barriers to effective communication/ understanding)

How do you apply approaches to understanding? In this context, applying various approaches, depending on who you are dealing with, means that you should use different methods to be able to understand them better. As people go through different phases in their lives, while interacting with them, it will be helpful to consider what phase of their life they are in, to facilitate understanding.

To maintain any kind of relationship with someone, it is important to understand that it takes patience, and that patience will help us to better understand the people we associate with.

Here's a hypothetical situation that might arise; you are dealing with a person, and there is an unfortunate misunderstanding. Suppose you are close friends with this person and feel you should address the issue. A variety of approaches will be beneficial. If one method doesn't work, an alternative can be tried. The more ways that we employ to deal with issues, the more chances we have to be able to understand. This, of course, depends on how much you value the kind of relationship you have with the other person. Not all relationships are worth nurturing. A connection with every single person may be impossible. What matters is that we show respect, even if we are not close or connected with people.

3. Communicating and Listening

Communication can open many doors to understanding. We are essentially trying to understand others when they are communicating with us, so it is vital to actively listen to them as best as possible. There's a lot of information that could be obtained when paying attention to the people we are interacting with. Have you ever been around people, and while communicating with them, although it's clear they can hear you speaking, they are not paying attention? This makes the information you are conveying to them seem somewhat irrelevant.

When interacting with others, it would be helpful to allow ourselves to listen carefully and connect with the information that is being provided. That would allow you to understand and relate to them better. Though it is crucial to understand others, you can only gain a full understanding of them when the person you are interacting with provides enough information. Therefore, trying to get as much information as possible will be helpful.

4. Try to Avoid Placing Expectations or Assumptions on Others

Assumptions and expectations can lead you away from trying to understand others. Aside from the value placed on a relationship, there are possible factors that can affect the effectiveness of any approach to understanding the other person. The focus will be on expectations and assumptions and how they impact our interactions.

What does it mean when expectations or assumptions influence approaches to understanding others in this context? The expectation of understanding occurs when we feel others should understand, while the assumption occurs when a person has already decided on what others should understand without receiving any clarification. It would be beneficial to our relationships to try to avoid have assumptions and expectations on others when trying to understand. Therefore, allowing others to express themselves as they are.

5. Understanding is influenced by expectations

Have you ever been in a situation where someone had no understanding of you as a person or the situation you were experiencing or vice versa? Do you think they understand you in a more general sense rather than based solely on your identity? Perhaps the person you are dealing with has unrealistic expectations of how you should understand him or her and how he or she should understand you. Although there are benefits to having expectations in some areas of life, like setting personal goals for motivation, expectations could negatively affect any relationship when it comes to attempting to understand others.

When it comes to understanding, expectations can put pressure on how you want people to think or behave. Having meaningful relationships with others is impossible if things don't evolve organically. Understanding others requires understanding who they are, because it can be helpful to apply different approaches. We can establish stronger relationships when we acknowledge that we all interpret things differently and have different expectations. You may have dealt with someone and understood something immediately; however, the situation with another person may not have the same outcome. Therefore, by trying to apply patience, we can truly understand each individual based on what we know about him or her and the way we understand them.

Different factors contribute to how people perceive things, which can impact their understanding. One main factor, I will talk about later in this book, is *'Perspective'* which plays a crucial role in our relationships. Considering its acknowledgement, we can use several approaches to understand others and, of course, this will require patience to try other approaches. To maintain any relationship, effort and commitment are needed. Any successful relationship requires hard work from both parties and maintaining your valued relationship will require renewed effort.

Expectations are putting your standards on how you think one should understand, which means wanting people to understand based on your wishes. If you place expectations on others, it could mean that you want them to perceive things the way you would. Expectations prevent you or others from having a natural experience in any kind of relationship. The reactions, emotions, and perceptions of people are beyond our control. Thus, having expectations about how people understand could affect our happiness. One element of understanding others is letting go of expectations while remaining open to different responses. Taking responsibility for ourselves means acknowledging that we only have control over ourselves.

6. Understanding Can Be Affected by Assumptions

The process of comprehending a person may not always go according to plan when we make assumptions about them. Finding clarity is beneficial because there is a possibility that our conclusions may be incorrect. By making assumptions, we can create misunderstandings. Therefore, assuming things without facts can lead to misunderstandings, misjudgements, and even confusion. To better understand someone, it is important to reduce assumptions and deal with facts. Imagine, for example, that you want to do something with someone but have decided its outcome because of how long you have known them. There is a possibility that familiarity will play a role. The moment you assume something, you already anticipate how it will be interpreted. That could lead to many misunderstandings.

Assumptions also prevent us from understanding things for what they truly are but what we perceive to be true. Many things could lead to us assuming when it comes to understanding. Among these reasons may include certain past events in their lives, which may be based on their past experiences. It could be negative, or positive but past events sometimes can make us assume when we are dealing with people.

You may not be dealing with the same person, you may be dealing with someone else, but what you've experienced with other people may affect your interactions with them and your assumptions about the person you're currently dealing with. For example, Diana had just left a relationship and her experience was that her ex-boyfriend was untruthful. She is now in a new relationship and already assuming that her new boyfriend will most likely also be untruthful. This is a sign that Diana is already putting barriers on her new relationship due to her assumptions from past experience.

In Diana's case, she lacks the understanding that her way of thinking could harm her new relationship. Even more so, what is causing Diana to assume that her new boyfriend will be untruthful, as she's just getting to know him? Maybe Diana has not healed from her last relationship? Or does she need more time to find herself again? Whatever the situation, one thing that stands is that her 'assumption' will most likely not allow her to open up to explore her new relationship, as she has already put a wall up against the new relationship and blocked any opportunity to understand the person she is currently with.

If you find yourself assuming during interactions with others, what are some of the reasons why you see yourself assuming? Try to note them down, especially when dealing with other people, to learn more about why you assume things and see if your reasons are valid. If possible, I suggest that you communicate your feelings to the people you are dealing with for clarity.

Here's another example

Jason and Darren have been best friends for many years. Since they are familiar with each other, Darren tends to assume things often when they interact. Jason does not ask Darren for clarification since he feels he can assume his answers given the length of time they have known one another. As a result, there have been some misunderstandings between them. These misunderstandings have led to their relationship deteriorating, as Darren finds it increasingly uncomfortable to deal with him. In this case, familiarity is the cause for the assumption. It's possible that when we know someone too well, we see no need to explore further with them, and that's when it's called a *"too familiar relationship"*. This familiarity may also contribute to overconfidence.

It is possible to be overconfident at times when dealing with certain people in certain circumstances because we have been dealing with them for some time. Even if we know someone very well, or an event very well, we can never know a situation too well, regardless of whether it is new or not. As we deal with different people, it's important to remember they will respond to things differently.

Thus, assumptions can affect how we understand things. It is important to avoid assumptions when attempting to understand others.

Let's look further into assumptions and expectations. Here are some ways to consider managing expectations and assumptions about others in a positive manner so you can nurture relationships better, and by so doing, you will be more understanding.

Action Tips

Managing Expectations and Assumptions

Here are some things I've suggested to others and done myself in the past.

i) Managing Expectations

- **Acknowledging what is realistic and what is not realistic**

Try to understand what is realistic for the person you are interacting with. Having an open conversation with the person you are interacting with could help you achieve this.

- **Appreciate people for who they are**

Appreciate the uniqueness of people, rather than expecting them to act or respond in a certain way, keeping in mind that we are only in control of our actions. So, there will be less pressure on yourself and others during interactions.

- **Considering how others heal should not be an expectation**

Being hurt is a normal experience in interpersonal relationships. In any case, it is best to not try to set any expectations about how and when one should heal. Healing takes time and differs from person to person. Forgiveness and forgetting are essential steps in this process. To forgive is to let go of your right to hold someone accountable for their hurtful actions towards you. Additionally, forgiving removes any negative feelings that would upset you in the future. Also, forgetting is like removing any thought of the situation as if it never happened.

Does forgiving mean we automatically forget? Through research, I have come across many articles that state that the two are interconnected; but I feel it depends on the individual. As human beings, we have emotions, and these emotions dictate how we feel. This means that sometimes it brings remembrance, so forgetting completely can be difficult depending on the individual, but we can try to control how it affects us. Having self-control is possible through self-awareness. The ability to identify what triggers your emotions and how we respond to those emotions is important to our peace of mind.

ii) Managing Assumptions

- **Questions are helpful**

Asking questions instead of making statements we are unsure of will help us uncover the real reasons for something. For instance, not every person who goes to the gym wants to lose weight, or not every quiet person is secretive. If I find myself making assumptions, it is an indication that I need clarity. Asking questions helps me gain clarity. I try to ask as many questions as possible. People do things differently, and to understand them better, it would be helpful to ask the right questions. I am very appreciative of people who attempt to ask me questions to gain clarity, to avoid assumptions and misconceptions. It also shows me how much interest they have in our interactions.

- **There is no such thing as being 'always right'.**

Firstly, you could acknowledge that your assumptions are not facts; you might be wrong. Trying to accept the fact that everyone sees things differently is a good reminder. In some situations, involving the other person or acknowledging their viewpoints will be beneficial because your assumptions are based solely on your beliefs. Without facts, it is easy to misinterpret. A meaningful relationship is not always easy to find; therefore, it would be useful to remind yourself why the relationship is important and how you can manage and strengthen it.

- **Try your best to listen carefully**

As we interact with others, there is a possibility that we could miss some vital details, which could lead to a set of assumptions. Therefore, paying attention while interacting with others is beneficial.

- **Exploring reasons for your assumptions**

It would be helpful to note down the reasons for any assumptions you might make, maybe by formulating a question or statement. Then, try to clarify any questions with the person you are interacting with. Let's say you believe that Mary is angry with you because you believe that she is. What made Mary angry with me? This assumption statement can be changed into a question, why do I think she is angry with me? Then, if possible, ask Mary why?

7. **Accepting others for who they are and their part in Social Roles.**

People should be accepted and respected for who they are and what they do. Just as we accept ourselves and want others to accept us, it is important to understand that others should be accepted for who they are as well; it works both ways.

Accepting others lets you explore their uniqueness without placing expectations on them. Sometimes we expect things from others that do not connect with their reality. The way we define the world is how we see it, and that does not guarantee that others will see it in the same way. The fact that something works for one person does not mean it will work for everyone. You may also have different strengths and weaknesses than others and it is important to accept this without trying to find yourself in others. We can reduce the level of expectations if we can accept others for who they are. If you accept a person for who they are, you let them be who they want to be and nothing else. By allowing them to be who they are, you are most likely to have a more enjoyable experience with them and with less pressure on your interactions.

Relationships require us to accept each other for who we are as individuals. This is also a professional practice in a work environment as it involves respecting people's preferences. Being accepting of others helps us to understand them more as individuals. As a result, we can also accommodate their differences and have room for their opinions.

We live in a diverse world and are globally connected. Different people see the world differently, so if we can practice accepting others, it will help our relationships. The act of accepting others may seem straightforward on the surface, but sometimes it can be challenging to implement. As humans, it is in our nature to be a bit judgemental, and we all may have been judgemental one way or the other in our interactions with others. This can improve if we become more accepting of them.

Have you ever experienced being around people who always judge your way of doing things because it's not the same as theirs or vice versa? Is there anyone in your life who constantly tries to change you, despite the fact that your actions do not affect them negatively? In some cases, family members (or those close to you) may want you to become someone you are not. It is not uncommon for people to hope that others will do things in the same way as them before they understand. The result is that people are stripped of their authentic selves. Remember, people aren't going to view things in the same way as we do. Let's allow people to thrive in their ways and be themselves, especially when it doesn't harm anyone.

Action Tips

How To Be More Accepting of Others

Here are a few ways to consider becoming more accepting and understanding.

• **Accept and Be Yourself**

It is helpful to ask whether we have accepted ourselves before attempting to accept others. If we cannot accept ourselves, we will find it much harder to accept others.

• **Acknowledge that Everyone is Unique**

We can be more accepting when we acknowledge that we are all different. Having different interests and doing things differently is normal. Seeing people as unique individuals enables us to interact with them or keep them in our lives as well as to accept their qualities and the way they do things, etc. Depending on the person, they may be reserved, shy, introverted, **or** talk a lot. Some people are introverts, while others are extroverts. It's not harmful to let them be who they want to be, as long as we can find ways that work for us to interact with each other.

Accepting differences is a better approach than complaining about them. It would be helpful to understand those differences or re-evaluate whether the relationship can continue.

If you are concerned about indifferences, you may consider these questions.

- Is the other person's behaviour physically, mentally, or emotionally harming me?
- Is it just a matter of hoping that people I interact with have the same personality as me?
- If the behaviour makes me uncomfortable, have I considered speaking up about it?
- Am I able to accept them for who they are?
- How would I feel if others complained about me even though it's not negatively affecting them?
- Can I acknowledge that the person can't be me and I can't be them?
- Am I seeking to have a natural experience with others, or do I want to have control over them?

Relationships in which one person feels their way is better and the other must behave the same should be avoided as much as possible. Additionally, we shouldn't make people feel bad for having different strengths or weaknesses. We aren't all able to do everything the same way; there will always be something another person is better at than you and vice versa. Comparing ourselves with others or shaming others for not having the same skill set as we do is not necessary. A meaningful relationship cannot be maintained if we bring people down because of all the differences.

• Not taking things personally and considering others

To not take things personally in this context, I mean sometimes the person is just being who they are and not doing that to make you feel uncomfortable. During my research, I interviewed two people with stories about how they felt less accepted. This was because some of their relationships suffered because of things about them that were taken personally most times.

■ *Christopher*

As he points out, his colleagues say he is not friendly at work, since all his conversations are work-related, and they'd like him to talk about things outside of work as well.

In this situation, his co-workers must accept that he is communicative, but prefers non-work-related conversations outside of work. To improve their interaction with him, it would be helpful to understand who he is as an individual without taking his behaviour personal.

- *Monica*

She prefers to keep her distance from others when she is down. She needs space to be alone for her to heal but people close to her feel like she does not appreciate them due to the distance and not asking for help. According to Monica, she is simply working through a process of healing and overcoming what she was going through. People close to her take it personally that she doesn't come to talk to them Occasionally, it can lead to them feeling as though they have wronged her.

This is another situation where it is important not to take things personally. Perhaps wanting space is her way of doing things and not aimed at making anyone feel uncomfortable.

The reason a person acts a certain way may not always be about us, but we can at times try to understand why a person behaves in that way without taking it personally. Firstly, it's unlikely that we'll find a person with every attribute we're looking for. We shouldn't try to find everything we need in one person because that person may not exist. **Different people will have different qualities we can relate to.** It will be challenging to find the perfect person. As individuals, we are not flawless;

therefore, expecting the perfection of others is neither fair nor realistic. For instance, not everyone in your circle of friends may find you funny, and vice versa.

People will have different qualities with which you can connect. If you are into sports, you will probably know a few people who also enjoy watching sports. It is possible that some people may dislike what you enjoy, while others may enjoy what you enjoy. What matters is that we accept their presence just as they are, as long as that does not harm us in any way. We must appreciate and connect with the traits we can connect with. You will also not possess every quality but will expect others to accept you. Everyone has a process in place as to what works for him or her or how they choose to live. Let us complement each other and be less judgemental but more understanding. This will allow relationships to flourish naturally. It is important not to take everything personally. Instead, we should learn to appreciate each individual's traits.

• Directing your Energy on People's Strengths

Are you often judged by people you interact with because of your weaknesses? Here's an example, Phillip isn't always straightforward in his communication style. Instead of judging him, perhaps understanding why he is the way he is will be more beneficial to helping you accept him better and thus understand him better. It will also help anyone with whom he interacts to know how to approach him and to better communicate with him.

Our strengths and weaknesses are all unique, and we may find it hard to accept others if we focus only on their weaknesses.

Key Reminders

- Being able to understand people with whom we interact with can help us strengthen our relationship with them.

- Flexible approaches would help us learn more about others, and in turn, benefit our relationships.

- Understanding can be hindered by expectations and assumptions, causing one's approach to understanding to be less flexible.

- There is a decent possibility that you will become a prisoner of your thoughts because you could be thinking about events or circumstances that are not true and might not allow your relationship to flourish organically.

- Assumptions could have a negative impact on how we relate and communicate with others because they make us think we already know why people do what they do and then draw our conclusions without knowing the facts.

- We can interact more effectively with others if we can manage barriers such as expectations and assumptions.

- Being open-minded will most likely be beneficial to our relationships and to help us develop positive relationships with others.

CHAPTER 3

UNDERSTANDING PURPOSE

"Remember that different people in your life are a collection of different adventures and you will experience different things with them"

W e all have a purpose in life. I feel that defining the word 'purpose' could mean different things for different people.

Different factors, such as upbringing, environment, beliefs, culture, etc. could influence how one may choose to understand and express themselves when talking about purpose. One thing I would say is, take some time in deep thought and visualise the way you are living now.

Ask yourself if this way of living makes you happy, positive, motivated, fulfilled, and is positively impacting others. If the answers are yes, then you may as well say that you're living your purpose. When you live purposefully, it can have a positive impact on your relationships as you are most likely to be content in your life, and that could improve how you relate to others. Research shows that those with a purpose paid more attention to their loved ones and communities.[6] Additionally, people with a purpose were most likely to enjoy satisfying relationships, which included families, colleagues, and neighbours.[7] This shows the positive link between our purpose in life and the relationships we form. How fulfilled are you with life and how is that impacting your relationships? Is there anything holding you back from discovering your purpose?

It would be beneficial in our relationships to understand that there is a purpose for everyone. Everything exists for a reason. If you have not discovered it yet, I hope you do because it adds a whole new meaning to life. That does not mean that your life doesn't have any meaning now, but it just adds a different flavour to it. Whatever the reason, each one of us is yet to discover it, if not already discovered. The most important thing is that we accept each other and understand that we each have a purpose that is unique to us.

We cannot change people because their purpose is different from ours. Just like how we take time to grow, it makes sense to allow others to grow and follow the path that works for them.

Have you ever wondered how living a purposeful life can impact your relationships? Let's see how living a purpose-driven life can do just that.

Living a Purpose-Driven Life

Once you get the sense of understanding who you are and living true to your purpose, the puzzling relationships that you struggle with could fall into place when you commit to it. Here are some of the reasons why I believe so:

o You become more focused in life

You tend to have clarity on your goals and objectives and your life choices become better, which also includes your relationships. For example, let me share my experience. Once I discovered my purpose, I noticed that certain behaviours had no value to me, whether from myself or others, so I am very selective of who I surround myself with. The type of people I seek for close relationships has become clearer to me which makes my interactions more meaningful. My purpose has become my daily, weekly, and yearly focus. I am more focused and committed.

o You become more positive around people

Some traits can cause blockages to maintain relationships. Some of these traits include jealousy, envy, malicious gossip, etc. Although these traits are part of human nature, if not controlled, they can affect our relationships. For example, when you discover and live your purpose, you are less likely to become envious of other people. Why? Because if their purpose has nothing to do with yours, then you do not need to envy what they have achieved in life. It would be rather better to stay focused and committed to your purpose. Hence, you become more satisfied with yourself rather than wishing to become something not meant for you and displaying negative traits.

o It gives you an overall view of your relationships

Living a purpose-driven life will help you to identify the types of relationships you wish to be a part of. These are the types of relationships that can help you to grow in line with your purpose. It could help you to live with integrity and get that feeling of what is right and what motivates you to build on it.

>>>> Please note that the above are just a few examples out of the many examples of how living a purposeful life can impact your relationships <<<<

I believe that it is implausible to meet a person with the same purpose as you. But there's nothing wrong with that. **Remember that different people in your life are a collection of different adventures and you will experience different things in life with them.** Some people will come into your life for various reasons but there will always be something unique to learn from them no matter what the purpose is. One thing you're going to realise is that when you get hold of that thing that makes you happy and that feeling of fulfilment, you should know that you have discovered your purpose. You will find that your purpose is your passion. For example, I interviewed Tim who expressed that he felt he was living his purpose. I spoke to Tim about his experience. According to Tim, he has discovered his purpose in life. He has worked as a bank manager for most of his employment life. He was a family man and was somewhat comfortable with his job, which was paying him well. However, before his day ended, he felt stressed and unhappy and most times his energy around his family and the people he interacted with was negative. He began to question himself for a move to make positive changes. According to what he said about his current situation, he discovered his purpose, which was completely outside most of the things he previously did. Instead, his purpose was to coach others to start new businesses and to flourish in life. I asked why he felt this way. He responded that he felt accomplished knowing he has made a positive impact in another person's life and is very happy with what he does which is naturally connected to who he is.

Every morning he is uplifted to make a change in another person's life. This has brought him so much joy and happiness and positively impacted the people he interacts with in general, as he is mostly happy, present, and content with himself.

>>>> *Please note that the above is just one example out of the many possible examples, and finding your purpose is not only tied to your career because each individual is different<<<<*

When it comes to living a purposeful life, what have you discovered about yourself and what do you know about the people you interact with? Some people may have a purpose to be an inspiration in the lives of others, to have the best paying jobs, help others, live a peaceful life, be role models to their children, etc. It all varies with each individual. I have been to at least nine countries, some in Europe, Africa, North America, and yet to visit other parts of the world; and most of the people I have encountered had a purpose. It is useful to understand your purpose and the purpose of others, which is helpful in interactions with them. You can then relate to them accordingly, and vice versa.

Some people may be fortunate to discover their purpose at a young age while others do so later in life. However, it would come down to how determined you are to discover yours. Some people may even be happy with their lives and wish not to look deeper into finding their purpose, but in the end, it is all the individual's choice on what works for them and makes their lives meaningful. In all of this, the one thing that stands out is, there will be many occasions where you will be the missing puzzle in another person's life. For example, you may be in someone's life to help them during difficult times. There may also be a time where, to another person, you may be seen as a negative influence, but in the end, it may be a lesson to improve your life.

We will all play different roles in the lives of others at different stages.

Let us seek the positive in any situation or the lesson it is teaching us. How accepting are you of others? Let us pay attention to how we are all unique in our special ways and appreciate each other.

Action Tips

Things I could consider applying to my life

○ I will explore more about myself authentically to find what makes me happy.

○ I will live in alignment with my true self.

○ I will acknowledge and understand that different people will play different roles in my life and vice versa.

○ I will respect that my 'whys' in my life will not be the same as others because we don't have the same purpose.

○ I will not impose my definition of 'happiness' on others and will allow them to define their own purpose.

Key Reminders

- Your purpose would improve your life choices and help you control the direction you wish to take.

- Discovering your purpose can add new meaning to your life but it also means different things to different people. Overall, it's supposed to make our general satisfaction of life better.

- It's important that we acknowledge and respect each individual's purpose and accept others for who they are. Accepting others, as highlighted earlier, does not mean to entertain situations that could harm our wellbeing. However, we have to respect ourselves first and respect other people's journey in life.

- It is also beneficial to understand that your purpose should be authentic to you, and something that works for you but not because others want you to do it.

- To discover your purpose, it should come from within, and not from outside. Having a purpose can improve your general wellbeing and will impact your relationships positively.

CHAPTER 4

UNDERSTANDING RESPECT

"When you respect yourself, you get a sense of self-acceptance of who you are, and that determines your worth"

Regardless of how close a relationship is, respect plays an integral role in it. When interacting with others, respect should be reciprocal. Disrespect can impact an individual or any form of relationship. No one wants to feel disrespected in any way and feeling disrespected can trigger many undesirable emotions. Let us take a journey into how respect can improve our relationships by starting with respecting ourselves first.

Self-Respect

For me, the concept of '*Respect*' is how a person shows a positive attitude and value towards another person or thing. It is essential to respect others; however, self-respect should come first. So, what is '*Self-Respect*'? The principle behind self-respect is that a person respects oneself which involves acceptance and appreciating their worth. Furthermore, to have self-respect is to value yourself. It is an essential ingredient in one's life because it aids in loving yourself.

Understanding respect and knowing how to extend it to yourself and others is an essential part of nurturing a relationship. The level of respect you give to yourself is most likely the level of respect you get from others.

When you respect yourself, you get a sense of self-acceptance and that determines your worth.

As mentioned in the previous chapter, self-acceptance does not mean you are perfect; however, you choose to accept your strengths and weaknesses. It means you respect yourself enough to acknowledge that although there are great things about you, you also have flaws that need working on. When you know all this, it adds value to who you are as an individual and makes you understand your worth without under-valuing yourself.

Self-respect is an internal process, and its outcome will reflect externally. This could help you select and maintain relationships that you feel you are worthy of.

Let us take a look at some ways to show respect to yourself which could impact your relationships positively.

Action Tips

Here Are Some Ways to Display Self-Respect

As I mentioned earlier, self-respect is an essential element of self-love. By encouraging ourselves to consider the following steps, we can improve our self-respect.

• Be more forgiving

To love yourself completely, it's important to forgive yourself for past mistakes. Holding on to resentments can prevent you from loving yourself the way you should. Hence, you must treat yourself better even while improving from lessons learnt. Being able to forgive yourself would also allow you to learn how to forgive others.

• Not to compare yourself to others

To show that you love yourself, it is vital to respect who you are without comparing yourself to others, especially in a shameful way or a way that brings you down. That is an easy way to kill your self-esteem and jeopardise your goals.

On the other hand, sometimes, a comparison may play a good role in our lives depending on how we apply it. Some positive ways of applying comparisons can be, for example, comparing yourself to a person with whom you may have similar goals and would like to emulate.

Comparing a particular skill might be beneficial to your growth but feeling jealous about others and not appreciating your whole being might be seen as disrespecting yourself.

If someone wishes to benchmark their goals against others, this would be advantageous, but to try to be someone else completely will be challenging. Comparing yourself to others in a toxic way can impact how you feel about yourself, which could also affect how you behave around others.

- **Be authentic with yourself and others**

If you want others to respect you, being authentic is one of the essential ways to go.

What does it mean to be authentic in this context? It means to be the person you want to be, but not what others expect of you. The picture of what others want you to be would most likely lead you to unhappiness. Self-understanding is one of the ways to be authentic. You will be happier if you respect yourself rather than seeking approval from others. What others want you to be should not define who you are or what you want in life. Believing in yourself boosts your confidence and would influence how you present yourself to others, which can help them understand you better.

- **Take responsibility for your actions**

One way to show respect to yourself is to accept responsibility for your actions. This again falls under accepting your weaknesses, which can sometimes be the mistakes we make. Accepting our mistakes is a form of self-respect as it shows that we have learnt from them and are looking forward to making improvements. This is a positive factor in respect and responsibility. You are most likely to be trusted if you respect yourself enough to be accountable for your actions. This will also help your relationships get better.

• Be Humble

Humility and respect are co-dependent (connected); hence, being humble can be a way of showing respect to yourself and others. What does it mean to be humble, and how is it linked to respect? You become respectful when you practice humility. Some of the qualities of a humble person are as follows:

- Treating people as you would want to be treated
- Exercising patience
- Being open to growth
- Not judgemental of others
- Being appreciative

• Set healthy boundaries

Firstly, what are boundaries? Setting boundaries mean drawing the line between what you can manage in your comfort zone and how you want others to treat you.

If you have a deeper understanding of yourself, it will guide you to what boundaries to set. For instance, we don't have control over what others do, but we can attempt to manage how we respond to them. For example, if I am communicating with a person and they are not polite, I can put a boundary in place by choosing to only continue the conversation if they are polite. If you don't set boundaries, you will end up consuming so many unnecessary things that will drain your energy and make you feel disrespected.

It is important to know when to say 'no' to situations that don't serve any positive purpose to your well-being. Ideally, boundaries that are clearly communicated to people can help set the platform to manage what behaviour you will accept from them in terms of how they treat you.

You exhibit self-respect by putting these boundaries in place. It can strengthen your relationships as you have communicated how to be treated. People who are aware of themselves are likely to communicate how they wish to be treated and to set healthy boundaries.

Setting healthy boundaries means making the other party aware of what you stand for. That way, they are aware of what you will not tolerate and vice versa. That's one-way others can respect you because they understand your values and self-worth. Also, you set boundaries when you try to identify what role you play in each person's life, so then you will know how to behave around them.

Have you defined and communicated your boundaries? It's something worth doing to help your interactions to be equally respected. The next subheading goes into detail about respecting others.

Respecting others

One of the ways we can display self-respect is to respect others. Respecting oneself will allow us to see the essence of respect in general, so as we practice respecting ourselves, the ability to respect others will follow. We all have a chosen way of living to thrive, and in life, many events may happen. Some may be positive and others negative, but in the end, we are all trying to figure out what this thing called 'life' is about and how we can accomplish our goals and thrive. It will be essential to our relationships to understand the importance of allowing people to live their lives in a way that works for them, especially when it doesn't harm us in any way. Understanding to respect others may come in various ways. This could include learning to respect people's:

❖ privacy

- ❖ choices

- ❖ views

- ❖ feelings

- ❖ career path

- ❖ relationships

- ❖ family life

- ❖ values

- ❖ lifestyle

- ❖ beliefs

Aside from harmful situations, it is ideal to understand that there is nothing wrong in agreeing with others, whether it has to do with their views, choices, or feelings. We can respect all these things and accept that it is different from ours. That should not mean anyone is right or wrong. What it simply means is, we can accept and respect each other for who we are.

Have you noticed that sometimes people choose to respect other people based on what they know about them or what they have heard about them? For example, people's level of education, the type of job they do, their past experiences, level of wealth, etc. These are all barriers to creating or maintaining meaningful relationships with others.

Action Tips

What are some of the things that the people you interact with find disrespectful? Do they communicate their boundaries clearly to you? Consider some of the following ways to become more respectful of others and to strengthen your relationships.

Some of the Ways We Can Show Respect to Others

- Apologise when you are wrong

- Try to listen carefully when others are communicating with you

- Don't always make it about you

- Don't undervalue their needs

- See their worth

- Get clarity on what they find disrespectful

- Accept their uniqueness

- Treat them fairly

- Be considerate of their feelings

- Show your gratitude for their time

>>>> Please note that the above are some examples that could be considered when seeking to respect others, although they will differ from individual to individual. <<<<

Key Reminders

- To be able to practice respect towards others, respecting ourselves first is one way to go.

- Keeping a healthy relationship will require respect, and it could strengthen your relationships to set some form of boundaries. It's important that as most people see the world through different lenses, trying to acknowledge and respect who they are can impact your relationships positively.

- People can change over time because of the experiences they have had, but they should be respected for their differences, especially when they mean no harm to you.

- Learning to accept and respect others in the same way that you want others to respect you is the key. It's important to remember that the level of respect we give ourselves determines the level of respect we receive from others.

CHAPTER 5

UNDERSTANDING MINDSET

"Your life is a summary of your mindset"

Firstly, let's get a quick understanding of the meaning of *'mindset'*. A mindset is a set of beliefs that shapes the way you view the world and yourself. It impacts how you think, feel, and behave in a variety of situations.[8] Thus, what you believe about the world and yourself is expressed through your mindset.

The way we think has a link to almost everything we do or feel. Thus, our life is a summary of our mindset.

It has an impact on how we see ourselves, view others, and look at the world in general. Our general satisfaction with life will have an impact on our mindset. Therefore, it is vital to understand ourselves and others, and how our mindsets influence our interactions. Let us look further into Mindset.

Mindset – Growth, and Fixed

American psychologist, Carol Dweck, has classified that one can have a Growth and Fixed mindset.[9] Thus, to have a fixed mindset means that one can acquire their goals based on fixed traits/abilities, and to have a growth mindset means that one can have traits/abilities that, in time, their capacities or talents can be improved.[10]

I believe that most people might have a mixture of both mindsets, which could be applied depending on the situation. However, when it comes to relationships, I believe that a growth mindset will be more appropriate. To have a growth or fixed mindset is more like having either a closed or open mind.

The advantage of cultivating an open mind is that it provides access to a variety of opportunities. Regarding our relationships, having an open mindset will allow us to explore more options and provide effective opportunities to learn more about ourselves and others.

For example, having an open mind can allow you to explore various ways to overcome a challenge or seek different options to understand others; however, a fixed mindset would do the opposite.

It is common for individuals to base their actions on their emotions rather than their mindset. By this, I mean, it would help if we controlled our thoughts as it could impact our feelings. We can control our thoughts by being more aware of ourselves. Emotions are part of human nature and play a significant role in every form of a relationship. Our emotions will have a profound impact on how we live our lives and interact with others, and every emotion has its own characteristics and adds meaning to our experiences.

So, for example, let's say Abbie could be in a situation where she feels let down by a friend and feels hurt. Let's just say, Abbie is angry with her friend. Abbie's anger can affect her decision-making or how to resolve the issue. Interpersonal communication is useful in this situation. How will Abbie resolve this if she's too deep into her emotions? Expression of emotion is a natural part of life. You have every right to let your feelings out. However, try not to let them get the best of you and to disrupt your relationships. It's not about denying your emotions, but acknowledging and responding to them in a way that positively impacts your emotional well-being and managing them to make your relationship flourish.

Research shows that how we feel has an impact on what we see.[11] If you feel negative and hold on to negativity when dealing with others, you will respond negatively. Our mindset plays a role in our relationships, which we can look into now.

The impact of our mindset

How does the impact of our mindset affect us? We can either have a positive or negative mindset. The mindset we have can either influence our success or failure in life. It can motivate or de-motivate us and also have an influence on how we relate to others.

Our thoughts could be powerful and may project into our lives. So, are you nurturing positive or negative thoughts?

Things can improve if you cultivate a positive mindset, even if you have to work hard at achieving it. It's better than having a negative mindset. If you can manage your mindset when dealing with others, you will have more control over certain situations. In general, with a positive mindset, you should be able to come up with a positive way to:

- thrive in life

- solve challenges

- overcome stressful moments

- work and build on relationships with others

- improve your general well-being

- help nurture a positive attitude especially in times of difficulties

- handle challenging moments with colleagues at work

Throughout life, we face challenges. Most people have dealt with challenges in different ways. Some of these challenges may come to define us and help us to discover some of our strengths and weaknesses. But do we always have control over the challenges we face?

One thing we can attempt to control is our way of thinking towards that challenge. A negative mindset towards a challenge will make us feel defeated by the challenge. It may affect our thinking when it comes to decision-making. If we are looking to make a positive decision, a positive mindset can influence it. A positive mindset will guide us to focus on a positive response in our interactions.

Now, let us look into how our mindsets towards others can help our understanding.

Our Mindset and Its Impact on How we Relate To others

Since our mindset is about our thoughts, it will influence how we deal with others. How do you process information when dealing with others? Would you say you tend to see things only from your perspective or do you acknowledge others'? Are you consistently nurturing a positive mindset when dealing with others? Since we only have control over our thoughts and not the thoughts of others, we can, at least, do our part by cultivating a positive mindset, especially in our response to various matters.

What can we do when dealing with others that have a negative mindset? Well, we are only responsible and accountable for our thoughts, as they influence our actions. Using myself as an example, let's say I am communicating with another person, the other person can either choose to respond negatively or positively, how they react is out of my control. I am not responsible for the mindset people choose to have towards me. My responsibility is to manage my behaviour appropriately when dealing with them, and how they decide to respond is their responsibility.

Dealing with a person that has a negative mindset will be a difficult task, but at the end of the day, as previously highlighted, we have no control over how another person thinks. We can only focus on our part, and hopefully, what we can do to impact others positively. Sometimes, what we do positively exerts positive energy around others, which can influence others in a good way. Therefore, it is important to focus on working to create a positive mindset for ourselves first; that way, we exert positivity onto others and also set good examples.

When dealing with others, our mindset can either create solutions or problems, depending on where our focus is. For example, let's presume we had a misunderstanding. Most times, when we feel misunderstood, we somehow become defensive. Then we start exchanging words to prove a point. This is where the word "ego" comes to play its role in our relationships. Ego to me is what a person thinks about themselves and their worth. Ego can have its negative or positive impact on the relationships we form and on us. We can make ego a friend or an enemy depending on how we apply it to the relationships we form. For example, I use ego to motivate myself to achieve better results. However, whenever I am dealing with others, I need to put aside my ego. Ego can be seen from two perspectives, in my opinion. It can make us:

- feel like we are better than someone else

- feel like we are always right

- inconsiderate of the feelings of others

- have too much pride to see our mistakes

- always want to prove a point in an unhealthy way

- not accountable for our actions.

Let's be honest; we all have a certain amount of ego. That ego could make us defend ourselves to prove a point instead of focusing on fixing the issue and sustaining the relationships. It's important to have control over our ego, especially in times of conflict. Instead of focusing on what is right, we tend to put so much energy into proving who is right, which can go on forever. This is because who is right will mean different things to many people, but let's focus on what is right for the relationship itself.

What is right for the relationship is for a goal to succeed. For example, two friends might be in a conflict, and each one of them is trying to prove who is right, but ideally, the only thing beneficial for their friendship is what is right. The same thing applies to other relationships. This way, the focus is not on individual perspective, but rather, the type of relationship you are in as a whole. Remember, relationships can either succeed or fail. However, one constant thing is that success will come with mistakes, and we need to make sure we don't let our egos get in the way. The mistakes will guide us to the steps we must take to improve what we are not getting right. Giving up due to mistakes would put an end to a relationship that might have worked. However, the nature of the situation can also influence this decision.

Therefore, regardless of the form of relationship you are in, it's important to have a mindset that will seek solutions rather than create more problems unhealthily. Let us look into nurturing a positive mindset to help us find solutions to maintain our relationships

.

Action Tips

How to Nurture a Positive Mindset

As was highlighted earlier, humans are not perfect and do not always have a 100% perfect moment. We are faced with challenges, trials, negativity, let-downs, disappointments, etc. Although we all have different strategies to tackle such things, one thing that can make a big difference is a positive mindset.

Having a positive mindset may not change whatever we encounter, however, it may, at least, help us positively manage things. A negative mindset towards anything will give us a negative outcome. If we are looking to nurture a positive relationship with others, a positive mindset is one way to achieve that. In terms of understanding and building stronger relationships, having a positive mindset can be transformational as it can assist in how we deal with matters we encounter and make better choices.

Here are some of the things we may consider when nurturing a positive mindset.

○ **Positive self-talk (Affirmations)**

What we tell ourselves will affect what we do. It will benefit us if we avoid negative self-talk, as that will draw us away from any positive outcome. Research suggests that people who practice positive self-talk may have mental skills that allow them to solve problems, think differently, and cope with hardship and challenges more effectively.[12] This can reduce the harmful effects of stress and anxiety. It makes it evident that positive self-talk can influence us and our relationships with others. The mind will produce whatever information we input.

Let us look at a few positive self-talk statements you can put into practice.

Positive Self-Talk Statements

- I will create my own happiness.

- I will not allow my mistakes to draw me away from my purpose; I am stronger than my challenges.

- How I see myself is very important.

- I will focus on the lessons learnt from my mistakes rather than dwell on the problems.

- I choose to make respecting myself a priority.

- I am grateful for all I have while I work towards my goals.

- I choose to have a positive mindset to help me understand others better.

- I choose to work hard on my relationships.

o **Be Open-Minded**

Being open-minded helps you explore more in whatever situation you may find yourself in, rather than being closed-minded, which prevents you from finding various ways to look at things. In all areas of life, it will be helpful if one can be open-minded. It allows growth and development.

How can we embrace growth and understanding without being open-minded? Things around us change and people tend to change from time to time. How are we adapting to this change? Being open-minded can be beneficial, especially when it comes to understanding and dealing with others. It also facilitates communication.

One may ask, 'So, should I prioritise open-mindedness in my relationships with others?' Well, in my opinion, it's entirely up to you and what you wish to gain from that relationship. Ask yourself, what do I wish to gain from this relationship? Are you looking to develop and grow, or are you happy maintaining things as they are? People want different things, and different things work for everyone. What may seem right to you may not seem right to another. As long as what we are doing is not harming anyone, we make choices suited for our relationships with others. Ultimately, an open-minded person is more likely to deal with situations better.

○ **Surround Yourself with Positivity**

Relationships can be assets or liabilities. What do I mean by that in this context? In this context, seeing a relationship as an asset means it could bring you progression, and seeing a relationship as a liability means it could draw you back in life.

Not all relationships are for us, regardless of the form. Some relationships can impact our well-being negatively. Having mentioned this, are you in a relationship, which you can classify as an asset or liability? I find this very important because who or what you surround yourself with can either positively or negatively impact you. There's a lot of energy in our surroundings, which can influence us, especially in the way we think. Sometimes, we don't even realise it, but it happens.

Our surroundings have an impact on us. Therefore, it is important to be around people who bring out the best in us. Bad energy can rub off on us when we surround ourselves in such situations. It can also drain our energy, which can be exhausting.

Research shows that surrounding yourself with negativity can influence you negatively.[13] As negativity is contagious, surrounding yourself with negativity will affect your mindset and how you deal with issues. Therefore, it will be beneficial to try to surround yourself with positivity if you are looking to nurture a positive mindset that will help you in your various relationships.

Being selective of whom and what we surround ourselves with can have a positive or negative influence on us. Let us choose wisely and be more aware of our surroundings and environment.

○ **Acceptance of the Reality**

As mentioned in the previous chapter, acceptance is taking things the way they are. Now, let us look at its connection with nurturing a positive mindset. We already know that nurturing a positive mindset can help us handle challenges. Have you seen yourself in a situation where you are in disbelief? How did you deal with it and how did it affect you?

When you find yourself in any situation, it would be helpful to, at first, try to have a positive mindset. You will need to accept the situation to help you work towards how you would wish to solve it. Resisting acceptance may be geared towards a negative mindset. We may lose control of a situation if we resist acceptance.

Sometimes, when we are unable to accept a situation, it leads to negative self-talk. Let's say you have had a very bad argument with a family member and later realised your disbelief of the situation. Because you have not accepted the situation, you may see yourself engaging in negative self-talk like, "I can't believe he/she did this, hence, I will not do anything about it". But a person who has accepted it will most likely say things like, "Yes, I know we had an argument, but I value my relationship so let's talk it out and find a solution".

I have spoken to people who had some situations where they were defeated by a challenge because they didn't accept the situation. They just didn't want to believe it was true. How did that affect their attitude? Of course, they couldn't do much. They were far from implementing a positive mindset because they refused to accept anything.

The only time they saw a positive difference was when they embraced acceptance. This was achieved by controlling their emotions. It motivated them to find solutions, and they were in control of the situation. Having control didn't necessarily mean they would be the one to solve the issue, but it guided them in the right direction. Sometimes, they would work towards the solution, and other times they would seek assistance.

As stated previously, we don't always have control over what happens in our lives. A positive mindset can help cultivate a positive attitude. Acceptance doesn't define whether what we have to deal with is right or wrong, but it just makes us accept the reality for what it is so we can work on transforming the situation if needed.

This, in turn, will help us stay in control of our lives and how we relate to others.

○ **Practise Self-Care**

Practising self-care is vital in taking care of your physical and mental health. Self-care is taking a break from your regular activities. To be in a positive state of mind, one of the most important ways is to take care of yourself. Our well-being is our priority. There are various forms of self-care, and it will mean different things to different people. Here are just some examples of things people may consider as self-care activities:

- physical exercise

- reading

- going for a walk

- listening to music

- taking a break

- making sure they have time for themselves

- eating healthy

- going on vacation

>>>> *Please note that the above are just some examples out of the many examples when it comes to self-care activities; different people have different activities that work for them* <<<<

Key Reminders

- Our mindset is critical to how we think and see the world. It impacts how we manage our relationships with others and ourselves.

- To create positive relationships, our mindset towards other people is important.

- How often we cultivate positive thinking can make a difference.

- Just as we are not perfect, we shouldn't expect perfection from other people.

- Nurturing positive relationships doesn't necessarily mean we must cultivate perfect relationships.

- It means we must have a positive attitude to cultivate healthy relationships with a positive mindset.

CHAPTER 6

UNDERSTANDING PERSPECTIVE
(TAKING THINGS INTO PERSPECTIVE)

"Your viewpoint is important, but it is also important to consider the point of view of others because that's their perception of the world and reflects their outlook on life"

Regardless of the form of relationship we nurture, it is important to have a mindset that allows us to consider *'perspective'* when dealing with others.

The APA dictionary of psychology defines 'perspective' as the ability to take into consideration and potentially to understand themselves and others.[14] Our perception impacts our perspective. Thus, *'perception'* is about the interpretations of things. It is common for misunderstandings to occur because a perspective is not taken into account.

Here is my experience of perspective. It taught me to be selective about the relationships I establish. Why? Because interacting with others will be difficult if they refuse to be informed about perspective. It is one of the factors that could strengthen my relationships. Particularly in times of misunderstanding, I believe that perspective is of crucial importance.

When it comes to understanding ourselves and understanding others, it's a broad subject as many areas could be explored. However, for the purpose of looking into nurturing meaningful relationships, the main focus will be the perception of life and handling conflicts and disagreements, as those two factors can impact our relationships. Also, we can make a positive change to our relationships if we understand this concept.

Perspective and Conflicts/Disagreements

The world population is over 7.8 billion.[15] From this figure, it is highly unlikely that we will meet anyone who does and sees things in the same way that we do or has experienced everything we have. That is why it is important to pay attention to perspective.

When it comes to conflicts or disagreements, having the appropriate mindset, we should be able to manage how we deal with negative situations. Conflicts or disagreements in any form of a relationship is inevitable as it's part of life. We are going to find ourselves in a conflict or disagreement with others, whether at work, school, at home with a partner or spouse, or even with family members.

You are going to have many difficulties with others who are dedicated to not respecting your perspective and that could make it difficult to maintain a relationship with them. I can only imagine how you feel when the people you communicate with don't acknowledge your perspective.

Throughout the chapters, I have stated how different things like our values, beliefs, upbringing, etc., influence our way of doing things, and these things are linked to our perception of the world. Let us look at it this way; as children, we were taught to look left and right before crossing the road. Looking at just one side before crossing can lead to a problem.

That is how I see perspective. It is always important to consider both sides before taking an action. If we want to nurture positive relationships with others, it will be a good idea to consider their views. The ability to consider the perspective of others doesn't necessarily mean someone is right or wrong, but it allows us to respect their views when interacting with them.

Have you noticed that most times, when people argue, it's probably because they feel they are right? It's not uncommon that we may fail to understand that what works for one person might not work for another and vice versa. That's why keeping an open mind will help the relationships we form.

It is crucial to have a positive mindset when dealing with others. Having a negative perspective means cultivating negative thoughts instead of positive ones. Negative perspectives will give us a negative attitude towards a situation. As previously mentioned, we can't always control what event comes our way, but we can attempt to cultivate a positive perspective to help us gain a positive attitude towards the situation.

How do you respond to challenging events that occur in your life? Although, sometimes, it may look bad, how we interpret it may create a positive difference. Let's say you are in a difficult situation; the question is, are you looking to be defeated by it or looking to overcome the situation? Do you have a mindset that perceives problems or solutions?

The answer lies in how you choose to perceive the situation. Most times, our perspective of a situation has an impact on our interpretation. Just like the mindset we cultivate in our relationships; our perspective impacts our quality of life. What are some of the ways perspective can be applied to our lives?

Action Tips

Applying Perspective

During a conflict or disagreement, do you ever wonder or ask the other person how they view the situation to try to have an idea of the meaning behind their actions? You avoid making judgments about others or drawing conclusions that don't match their reality when you apply perspective to your interactions to understand their perspective.

Your viewpoint is important, but it is also important to consider the point of view of others because that's their perception of the world and reflects their outlook on life.

If we see things from the other person's perspective, we allow ourselves to understand their actions, emotions, or behaviour better.

Let us look at ways we can consider applying perspective to improve our relationships.

- **Communication (asking questions)**

Communication is one of the best ways to gather and convey information. One thing I have realised is that we have our interpretation of what we want as individuals, and society has its interpretation of what it makes us think we want. We will relate to each other better if we communicate what we want. The information we collect can help us understand one another better. Asking questions can help to get clarity on another's perspective. It is also important to communicate to understand definitions.

For example, a friend can tell another friend, 'You are not being a good friend lately'. It helps to clarify what 'being a good friend' means to them. There are some basics of what "being a good friend" means; however, it is still vital to communicate your exact needs to each other. That way, you can be more specific on how to relate to each other. We must ask further questions if it's not clear enough, and it would be helpful for the other party to have enough patience to give information to help in the understanding process.

Another important point is to focus on dealing with relationship issues with the parties involved. You have to be careful about making outsiders the first point of contact when there's a misunderstanding; whether it's with family or friends. Other people's interpretation of your relationship will not be as accurate as your own.

Their perspective will simply differ, which could lead to more misunderstandings. Therefore, questions should be directed as much as possible to the relevant person.

- **Exercise patience**

Patience can be applied to many areas in life. In this context, what I mean by exercising patience is taking time to understand each other and iron out indifferences. Trying to see things from the other person's perspective might not always come easy for most or all; however, through communication, one might need to apply patience to understand them better. Using patience will not only help you gain insight from the other person's perspective, but it will also show to the other person(s) that you are interested in learning more about them to help your relationship grow.

- **Being objective**

Being objective means not seeing things from your experience or past situations but dealing with the facts. If we want to see from the other person's perspective, then it will be helpful not to mix our personal feelings or emotions as we are not trying to understand ourselves, but the focus should be on the other person.

- **Being Empathetic**

Being empathetic means understanding how others feel; so, it's simply trying to put yourself in the shoes of others. Empathy can strengthen our ability to see things from the other person's perspective.

Key Reminders

- Interacting with others is not a process for one person, but it involves others, and, naturally, each person would like to be understood.

- Relationships have a sense of meaning when we consider the perspective of others.

- Considering the perspective of others in any form of relationship will help the way we interact and also strengthen our relationships. Communication becomes central to understanding the other person's perspective and is vital.

- We don't need to have the same perspective, but we can, at least, acknowledge and respect each other's viewpoint to strengthen and maintain our relationships.

- We all live in the world but what we see is what is around us, and that influences our interpretation of life, which gives us our perspective.

- It's okay for people with different standpoints to be right about the same situation and having a perspective doesn't mean we are obliged to agree or change someone else's but to use it as a guide to understand them better and to maintain your relationship with them.

- We can still have a good relationship with others without having identical perspectives as long as we respect and accept others for who they are.

CONCLUSION

*C*reating relationships may or may not come easy to some people but maintaining these relationships could be challenging due to the complexity of life and indifferences. Relationships, in general, formed with friends, family, and acquaintances in an educational or work environment need attention. Relationships have a chance of survival if we place value on them and work to nurture them to become meaningful.

Any form of relationship is not perfect. We must create and nurture them to become meaningful. The value and effort we put into these relationships contribute to their success or failure. Therefore, it will help to consider a person's values, beliefs, way of thinking, lifestyle, and background, when interacting with them. So that when these interactions develop conflicts, we would know how to fix things without letting the relationship grow sour or end for good. We can learn to maintain these relationships, which we value, and not allow certain mistakes or faults to damage them.

The objective of this book is to highlight how we can nurture positive relationships through the art of 'understanding'. As we all may know, the human experience is quite complex. Our lives are filled with many things, whether they are work-related, family-related, or personal; and sometimes it is difficult to keep up with everyone, including ourselves.

We play many relationship roles at a time; one person may play the role of a mother, sister, friend, and colleague, or even a father, brother, and friend all at the same time. Therefore, the key is the management of these roles accordingly. All relationships, not just love relationships, need attention to grow. This title has explored how implementing understanding in our lives can make a positive difference without having to underestimate its importance.

It has also dwelled on various topics, which has drawn the attention of the impact of self-acceptance, applying various approaches to understanding, understanding purpose, understanding respect, and understanding mindset. These are a few out of the many topics associated with understanding that can make a positive change in our lives.

We can create a positive environment when understanding is applied effectively. Most of the problems we face in our relationships, somehow, have a link to misunderstanding. It will help to ask ourselves, are we forming relationships with the right people? Trying to be close with everyone around us instead of selecting whom we can connect with. Are we implementing the right strategies to understand one another, whether in our personal or professional lives? Are we appreciating each role that various people play in our lives instead of expecting them to be everything to us? These are some of the important questions to ask ourselves in whichever form of relationship we seek to nurture.

Understanding others and ourselves will be an ongoing journey that we will take with ourselves and with others. It will help us to discover new things about others and ourselves, have new goals and face new challenges in life. Thus, we have to relate to each other at the moment and grow with each other. Being able to grow with each other is going to strengthen our bond. We can manage ourselves by taking charge of how we respond and relate to others, but we can't manage how other people act or behave.

However, if we can't find anything, we cannot connect with another person to maintain a relationship;

maybe it's time we consider what that relationship means to us and why we are in it.

Regardless of whichever form of relationship it is, whether it's personal or professional, having an intention to make it succeed is a decision entirely down to each individual and understanding is one of the ways that holds a high priority. Perspective plays a crucial role in having a harmonious relationship. Regardless of the form of a relationship, it's normal that people may not have the same perspective but most likely have the same goal for a relationship and there are only two goals– to have a successful relationship or a non-successful relationship. One thing that stands is that success comes with mistakes so our relationships may come with ups and downs, but the goal is to work through each phase and not be defeated by the mistakes.

Understanding yourself and one another is a choice one will make based on the value of the relationship. That will be one of the main ways to help any form of relationship to stay strong.

I hope we can give ourselves a chance to be more understanding to explore more about others and ourselves.

I also hope this book has made a positive impact on your journey to being an understanding friend, coworker, partner, spouse, or family member to strengthen your relationships.

Key lessons to help nurture your relationships

- Understand that everyone is unique.

- Communication is vital for any form of relationship to flourish.

- It will be beneficial to our relationships to grow with each other.

- Nurturing a positive relationship will require consistency and commitment.

- A positive approach will give a positive result.

- Meaningful relationships require effort.

- Negative things happen, but with the right attitude, we can get positive reactions.

- If we want others to understand us, we must be willing to give them enough information to help them understand us better.

- Relationship goals can be mutual even with different perspectives.

- It's important to get clarity to understand each other's definitions.

- Nurture relationships where you feel accepted and appreciated.

R
E
M
I
N
D
E
R
S

- It is important to pay attention to the relationships we are in because not all relationships are for us.

- Most times, we fall out because of our flaws. Communicate your flaws to others not just your strengths

- Relationships flourish when all parties take initiatives to make it work.

A NOTE FROM THE AUTHOR

I would firstly like to thank you for purchasing this book and I hope you found it useful and impactful. If you are reading a book I have written for the first time, welcome to this journey of exploring how understanding can make a difference in our lives through different perspectives. Be sure to read 'Understanding is Underestimated' as well so you don't miss out on great content. I want to thank everyone who has already read my first title and is continuing this journey with me. I deeply appreciate your love and support. I hope this title will positively impact your life.

I believe we can transform our lives when understanding is applied effectively in our day-to-day lives. I hope as many people as possible will read this book and gain something positive out of it.

The subject '*Understanding*' is very close to my heart and I would love to hear from readers to know about your experiences with yourself or with others, during times where 'Understanding made a difference' or even experiences where you felt 'Understanding could have helped a situation you have been in.

I will be very delighted if you can recommend this book to others as I believe it can help many people. I also feel this book will be beneficial to book clubs for discussions, especially in the self- improvement area. *May understanding make a difference in your life.*

Kindest Regards,

Rosie Kendall

INVITATION

I would like to invite you to listen to my podcast series which focuses on various personal development topics which can help you improve the quality of your life. Below is the link.

https://anchor.fm/coachingwithrosie

ABOUT THE AUTHOR

Rosie Kendall is a Life Coach, an ESL teacher, and a financial crime expert, based in the UK, with a passion to help people discover their potential and excel in life. Rosie has a goal to empower men and women to transform the quality of their life. As a devotee of self-continuity, self-development and improvement, Rosie seeks to improve herself and take any opportunity to help others to fulfil their goals in life. Rosie also has a great interest in Life Skills and encourages others to make it a p r i o r i t y in their lives as it helps them adapt to challenges in life. She enjoys spending time with her daughter and travelling.

Rosie has a background in Psychology and Counselling through her studies and holds a BSc degree.

ALSO BY

ROSIE KENDALL

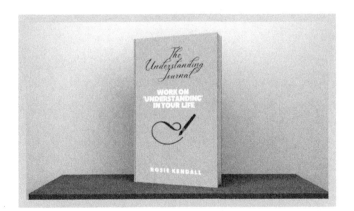

A SPECIAL REQUEST TO READERS

Your reviews and feedback mean a lot to me I would appreciate your honest reviews. This will also help others make an informed decision about this book.

THANK YOU.

Notes

[1] Melanie Greenberg, "Do Relationships Make Us Healthier and Happier?," Psychology Today, December 22, 2016, https://www.psychologytoday.com/gb/blog/the-mindful-self-express/201612/do-relationships-make-us-healthier-and-happier.

[2] Ronald E. Riggio, "Which Type of Perfectionist Are You?," Psychology Today, February 3, 2015, https://www.psychologytoday.com/us/blog/cutting-edge-leadership/201502/which-type-perfectionist-are-you.

[3] Thomas Curran, "The Problem with Perfection," London School of Economics, January 18, 2021, https://www.lse.ac.uk/research/research-for-the-world/health/over-stressed-and-under-pressure-the-problem-with-being-perfect.

[4] Anna Martin, "Understanding Self Acceptance," The Counsellor's Guide, last modified September 22, 2012, http://www.thecounsellorsguide.co.uk/understanding-selfacceptance.html.

[5] "How to Build Self-Acceptance," Mental Toughness Partners, September 2, 2018, https://www.mentaltoughness.partners/r-self-acceptance/.

[6] Barb Leonard and Mary Jo Kreitzer, "Why Is Life Purpose Important?," Taking Charge of Your Health & Wellbeing, accessed June 1, 2020, https://www.takingcharge.csh.umn.edu/why-life-purpose-important.

[7] Leonard and Kreitzer, "Why is Life Purpose Important?"

[8] Kendra Cherry, "Why Cultivating a Growth Mindset Can Boost Your Success," Verywell Mind, April 29, 2021, https://www.verywellmind.com/what-is-a-mindset-2795025.

[9] Gary Klein, "Mindsets," Psychology Today, May 1, 2016, https://www.psychologytoday.com/gb/blog/seeing-what-others-dont/201605/mindsets.

[10] Klein, "Mindsets."

[11] Association for Psychological Science, "The Emotions We Feel May Shape What We See," ScienceDaily, April 11, 2018, https://www.sciencedaily.com/releases/2018/04/180411090441.htm.

[12] Kimberly Holland, "Positive Self-Talk: How Talking to Yourself Is a Good Thing," Healthline, last modified June 26, 2020, https://www.healthline.com/health/positive-self-talk#benefits-of-self--talk.

[13] Jennifer Delgado, "Negativity Is Contagious: Surround Yourself with People Who Can Get the Best of You," Psychology Spot, accessed May 31, 2021, https://psychology-spot.com/positive-thinking-negative-people/.

[14] American Psychological Association Dictionary, s.v. "Perspective," https://dictionary.apa.org/perspective.

[15] "World Population Clock," Worldometer, accessed January 8, 2021, https://www.worldometers.info/world-population/.

Bibliography

Association for Psychological Science. "The Emotions We Feel May Shape What We See." ScienceDaily. April 11, 2018. https://www.sciencedaily.com/releases/2018/04/180411090441.htm.

Cherry, Kendra. "Why Cultivating a Growth Mindset Can Boost Your Success." Verywell Mind. Last modified April 29, 2021. https://www.verywellmind.com/what-is-a-mindset-2795025.

Curran, Thomas. "The Problem with Perfection." London School of Economics. January 18, 2021. https://www.lse.ac.uk/research/research-for-the-world/health/over-stressed-and-under-pressure-the-problem-with-being-perfect.

Delgado, Jennifer. "Negativity Is Contagious: Surround Yourself with People Who Can Get the Best of You." Psychology Spot. Accessed May 31, 2021. https://psychology-spot.com/positive-thinking-negative-people/.

Greenberg, Melanie. "Do Relationships Make Us Healthier and Happier?." Psychology Today. December 22, 2016. https://www.psychologytoday.com/gb/blog/the-mindful-self-express/201612/do-relationships-make-us-healthier-and-happier.

Holland, Kimberly. "Positive Self-Talk: How Talking to Yourself Is a Good Thing." Healthline. Last modified June 26, 2020. https://www.healthline.com/health/positive-self-talk#benefits-of-self--talk.

Klein, Gary. "Mindsets." Psychology Today. May 1, 2016. https://www.psychologytoday.com/gb/blog/seeing-what-others-dont/201605/mindsets.

Leonard, Barb, and Mary Jo Kreitzer. "Why Is Life Purpose Important?." Taking Charge of Your Health & Wellbeing. Accessed June 1, 2020. https://www.takingcharge.csh.umn.edu/why-life-purpose-important.

Martin, Anna. "Understanding Self Acceptance." The Counsellor's Guide. Last modified September 22, 2012. http://www.thecounsellorsguide.co.uk/understanding-selfacceptance.html.

Mental Toughness Partners. "How to Build Self-Acceptance." September 2, 2018. https://www.mentaltoughness.partners/r-self-acceptance/.

Riggio, Ronald E. "Which Type of Perfectionist Are You?." Psychology Today. February 3, 2015. https://www.psychologytoday.com/us/blog/cutting-edge-leadership/201502/which-type-perfectionist-are-you.

Worldometer. "World Population Clock." Accessed January 8, 2021. https://www.worldometers.info/world-population/.

Printed in Great Britain
by Amazon